Why Immigration Is A Good Thing

By James Hosie

1

Diversity Strengthens Societies Through Immigration:

One of the most compelling arguments in favor of immigration lies in its ability to infuse societies with a rich tapestry of perspectives, cultures, and talents. As individuals from different backgrounds come together, a diverse and vibrant social fabric emerges, contributing to the overall strength and resilience of a nation.

1. Enriching Perspectives: Immigration introduces a multitude of perspectives shaped by varying cultural, educational, and experiential backgrounds. This diversity challenges conventional thinking, fostering a more nuanced and comprehensive understanding of the world. Exposure to diverse viewpoints encourages open-mindedness and cultivates a society capable of tackling complex challenges through creative problem-solving.

2. Cultural Enrichment:
The infusion of diverse cultures through immigration creates a mosaic of traditions, customs, and artistic expressions. This cultural exchange not only enhances the daily lives of individuals but also contributes to a broader national identity that is inclusive and

celebrates the unique contributions of each community. Cultural diversity becomes a source of pride and strength.

3. Talent and Skills: Immigrants often bring a wealth of skills, talents, and expertise to their adopted countries. Whether in the fields of science, technology, arts, or business, diverse skill sets contribute to innovation and progress. The collaboration of individuals with different strengths leads to a more dynamic and adaptive workforce, positioning a society for success in an ever-evolving global landscape.

4. Social Cohesion:
While initially, the integration of diverse communities may pose challenges, over time, it fosters a sense of unity and shared identity. Interaction among people from different backgrounds promotes social cohesion, breaks down stereotypes, and builds bridges of understanding. Ultimately, a society that embraces diversity is more likely to foster tolerance, empathy, and a collective sense of belonging.

5. Economic Resilience:
A diverse workforce enhances economic resilience. Immigrants contribute to various sectors, filling gaps in the labor market

and supporting industries crucial for economic growth. This not only strengthens the overall economy but also ensures adaptability in the face of economic shifts and challenges.

In essence, the strength of a society is intricately linked to its capacity to embrace and harness the benefits of diversity through immigration. By fostering an environment where different cultures coexist, and varied talents converge, nations can build robust, adaptable, and culturally enriched communities that thrive in the modern global landscape.

2

Economic Contributions of Immigrants: Fueling Growth and Prosperity

The role of immigrants in shaping and propelling a country's economic landscape is undeniably significant. Their contributions extend across various facets, from labor to entrepreneurship and consumption, fostering robust economic growth. Understanding and appreciating these economic contributions is crucial for a comprehensive and nuanced perspective on the impact of immigration.

1. Labor Force Dynamics: Immigrants play a pivotal role in the labor market, often filling essential roles that contribute to the overall productivity and efficiency of various industries. They engage in a wide spectrum of occupations, from manual labor to highly skilled professions, addressing workforce gaps and ensuring the smooth functioning of sectors such as agriculture, healthcare, and technology. By participating in the labor force, immigrants not only contribute to the production of goods and services but also play a role in sustaining and expanding industries.

2. Entrepreneurship and Innovation:
Many immigrants bring with them an entrepreneurial spirit, establishing businesses that contribute to economic dynamism and job creation. From small enterprises to large corporations, immigrant entrepreneurs have made substantial contributions to local and national economies. Their ventures often introduce innovative ideas, products, and services, enriching the business landscape and contributing to a culture of innovation and competitiveness.

3. Consumption Patterns:
Immigrants are not just contributors to the production side of the economy; they also play a crucial role as consumers. Through their purchasing power, immigrants stimulate demand for goods and services, driving economic activity. This consumption contributes to the growth of various industries, from retail to housing, and creates a multiplier effect, generating additional employment opportunities.

4. Demographic and Fiscal Impact:

Immigrants, particularly those who arrive in their working-age years, have a positive impact on a country's demographic structure. They help address demographic challenges posed by aging populations by contributing to the labor force and supporting social welfare systems through taxes. Studies indicate that, on average, immigrants often contribute more in taxes than they receive in public benefits, debunking the notion that they are a drain on public resources.

5. Global Talent and Competitiveness:

Attracting skilled immigrants enhances a country's global competitiveness. These individuals bring specialized skills and knowledge, contributing to advancements in science, technology, and other critical sectors. By tapping into a global talent pool, nations can position themselves at the forefront of innovation, research, and development, ensuring sustained economic growth in a competitive global environment.

In conclusion, the economic contributions of immigrants are multifaceted and far-reaching. From labor that sustains industries to entrepreneurial endeavors that drive innovation, immigrants are integral to a nation's economic vitality. Recognizing and harnessing these contributions can lead to policies that promote inclusive growth and prosperity for both immigrants and the native population.

3

Demographic Balance through Immigration: Sustaining Societies in the Face of Aging Populations

As societies grapple with the challenges posed by an aging

demographic, immigration emerges as a pivotal solution to address these demographic imbalances. The infusion of younger, working-age immigrants not only bolsters the labor force but also plays a crucial role in supporting social welfare systems, ensuring their sustainability for generations to come.

1. Workforce Renewal:
One of the primary benefits of immigration in the context of demographic balance is the injection of vitality into the workforce. As native populations age and retire, the arrival of younger immigrants helps

replenish the labor pool. This influx of new workers is essential for maintaining productivity levels, sustaining economic growth, and preventing labor shortages in critical sectors such as healthcare, manufacturing, and technology.

2. Economic Contribution: Younger immigrants actively contribute to the economy by participating in the labor force. Their employment and income generation contribute to tax revenues, which, in turn, support social welfare programs. A growing and active workforce not only ensures the economic vibrancy of a nation but also helps alleviate the financial burden on social security and pension systems that would otherwise be strained by an aging population.

3. Social Welfare System Support:
Immigrants, particularly those who enter a country in their working-age years, become contributors to social welfare systems. Through the payment of taxes and social security contributions, they actively participate in funding programs that provide healthcare, pensions, and other benefits to the elderly. This financial intergenerational

support becomes crucial in maintaining the sustainability of social safety nets as the proportion of retirees increases.

4. Population Growth and Market Expansion:
Immigration contributes to overall population growth, helping counter the effects of declining birth rates. A growing population can stimulate demand for goods and services, fostering economic expansion. Additionally, a larger and diverse consumer base can lead to increased market opportunities, encouraging entrepreneurship and innovation.

5. Cultural Diversity and Integration:
Beyond the economic impact, immigration contributes to cultural diversity and integration. Young immigrants bring their unique perspectives, traditions, and skills, enriching the cultural fabric of a nation. The intermingling of different cultures fosters social cohesion, creating a dynamic and resilient society.

6. Long-Term Planning and Sustainability:
Countries that strategically incorporate immigration into their demographic planning demonstrate a commitment to

long-term sustainability. Policies that facilitate the integration of immigrants, provide education and training opportunities, and address cultural adaptation contribute to the successful incorporation of newcomers into the fabric of society.

In conclusion, immigration serves as a proactive strategy to mitigate the challenges associated with aging populations. By welcoming younger workers into the fold, societies can ensure a robust and balanced demographic structure, maintaining economic vitality and sustaining social welfare systems for the benefit of both current and future generations.

4

Innovation and Creativity Unleashed: The Immigrant Impact

Immigrants, with their diverse backgrounds and unique perspectives, serve as catalysts for innovation and creativity, propelling societies forward in the realms of technology, science, and culture. Their contributions, often shaped by a fusion of experiences and ideas, breathe fresh life into the creative landscape, fostering advancements that benefit society at large.

1. Cultural Fusion and Creative Crossroads:
Immigrants bring a wealth of cultural diversity, creating a rich tapestry of experiences. This cultural fusion becomes a breeding ground for creative crossroads, where ideas from different traditions intersect, giving rise to innovative solutions, artistic expressions, and novel approaches to problem-solving. This blending of cultural influences can be a driving force for creativity in various fields.

2. Technological Advancements:
In the technology sector, immigrants have played a pivotal role in driving advancements. Many successful entrepreneurs and engineers hail from immigrant backgrounds, contributing groundbreaking innovations that have shaped industries. Silicon Valley, for instance, stands as a testament to the impact of immigrant minds on the tech landscape, with numerous success stories rooted in diverse talent and ideas.

3. Entrepreneurial Spirit and Start-up Culture:

Immigrants often embody a strong entrepreneurial spirit. Their experiences of adapting to new environments and overcoming challenges foster resilience and a willingness to take risks. This entrepreneurial mindset contributes to the growth of start-up cultures, where new businesses driven by immigrant innovation emerge and thrive, generating employment opportunities and economic dynamism.

4. Scientific Research and Academic Excellence:
In academia and scientific research, immigrants make substantial contributions, bringing

fresh insights and perspectives to the pursuit of knowledge. Many Nobel laureates and leading researchers around the world come from immigrant backgrounds, showcasing the profound impact of diverse intellects on scientific breakthroughs and academic excellence.

5. Arts, Literature, and Cultural Expression:
In the realm of culture and the arts, immigrants infuse vibrancy and diversity. Their unique experiences often inspire works of literature, art, music, and film that resonate on a global scale.

Immigrant artists contribute to the evolution of cultural landscapes, challenging norms and introducing new narratives that enrich societies with fresh perspectives.

6. Global Collaboration and Exchange:
Immigrants, as bridges between different cultures and regions, facilitate global collaboration. The exchange of ideas and collaboration across borders accelerates innovation by bringing together diverse talents and resources. This interconnectedness fosters a global creative ecosystem where

breakthroughs benefit from a collective pool of expertise.

In conclusion, the contributions of immigrants to innovation and creativity are immeasurable. By embracing their unique perspectives and harnessing the fusion of diverse ideas, societies can propel themselves to new heights, driving technological advancements and cultural evolution. Recognizing and nurturing the creative potential within immigrant communities is not just a celebration of diversity but an investment in the continual progress of human ingenuity.

5

Global Interconnectedness through Immigration: Fostering Cooperation and Understanding

In an era marked by increased global interdependence, immigration stands as a testament to the recognition that our world is intricately interconnected. Embracing immigrants not only enriches societies locally but also contributes to a broader narrative of international cooperation, understanding, and shared humanity.

1. Recognition of Shared Humanity:
Embracing immigration underscores a fundamental acknowledgment of shared humanity. Regardless of borders and boundaries, people are connected by common aspirations, challenges, and dreams. The acceptance of immigrants reflects a commitment to viewing individuals as members of a global community, fostering empathy and solidarity.

2. Cross-Cultural Understanding:
Immigration serves as a powerful vehicle for cross-cultural

understanding. By welcoming individuals from diverse backgrounds, societies open themselves to a wealth of perspectives, traditions, and values. This exchange promotes cultural awareness and breaks down stereotypes, fostering a climate of tolerance and appreciation for the richness that diversity brings.

3. Diplomacy through People-to-People Connections:
The connections forged through immigration create invaluable people-to-people ties. These personal connections transcend political borders and serve as a

foundation for informal diplomacy. Individuals who have experienced life in different countries become ambassadors for understanding, promoting goodwill and positive relations between nations.

4. Economic and Social Networks:
Immigrants often establish economic and social networks that extend beyond national borders. These networks become conduits for trade, investment, and collaboration. As individuals maintain ties with their countries of origin, they contribute to a global web of relationships that

can foster economic development and international cooperation.

5. Mitigation of Xenophobia and Isolationism:
Welcoming immigrants challenges xenophobia and isolationist tendencies. It sends a powerful message that societies are open to engaging with the world, recognizing the benefits of diversity and collaboration. This openness counters the divisive forces that can arise from fear of the unknown and promotes a more inclusive, interconnected global community.

6. Response to Global Challenges:
Issues such as climate change, pandemics, and economic disparities are global challenges that require collective solutions. Immigration, with its inherent ties to global interconnectedness, positions societies to respond more effectively to these challenges. By fostering international cooperation, nations can pool resources, share knowledge, and address issues that transcend borders.

7. Educational and Intellectual Exchange:

Immigration facilitates the exchange of knowledge and intellectual capital. Scholars, scientists, and professionals who move across borders contribute to a global pool of expertise. This intellectual exchange not only advances research and innovation but also enriches educational institutions and industries on an international scale.

In conclusion, embracing immigration is not just a local policy but a statement about a nation's commitment to being part of a connected world. It reflects an understanding that our collective well-being is intertwined and that building bridges between cultures and nations is essential for a harmonious and prosperous global society. Immigration becomes a force that propels us toward a future where cooperation and understanding transcend borders, creating a world that truly embraces its interconnected nature.

6

Historical Contributions of Immigration: Enriching Societies Through Time

The historical tapestry of many successful societies bears witness to the profound impact of immigration. Across centuries, diverse populations have not only coexisted but have actively contributed to the prosperity and dynamism of their host nations. Examining historical patterns reveals that embracing immigration has been a key factor in the sustained development and enrichment of societies.

1. Cultural Mosaics and Civilization Building:
Throughout history, civilizations have flourished when diverse groups of people converged and

coexisted. The mingling of cultures, languages, and traditions often led to the creation of rich cultural mosaics. From the Silk Road connecting East and West to the cultural exchanges along the Mediterranean, historical immigration patterns have laid the foundation for the flourishing of art, philosophy, and technology.

2. Economic Booms and Innovation:
Many economic success stories are intertwined with historical waves of immigration. The Industrial Revolution, for example, saw mass migrations of people seeking employment in

burgeoning industries. These influxes of labor not only fueled economic growth but also contributed to technological innovation and the establishment of new markets.

3. Nation-Building and Infrastructure Development:
In the development of nations, immigrants have played crucial roles in building infrastructure and contributing to nation-building efforts. From the construction of railroads in the United States to the development of major cities worldwide, immigrants have been at the forefront of shaping the physical

and economic landscapes of their adopted homelands.

4. Scientific and Academic Advancements:
Historically, immigrants have significantly impacted the realms of science and academia. Notable scholars, scientists, and intellectuals often hailed from diverse backgrounds. Their contributions, whether in the fields of medicine, astronomy, or philosophy, have propelled societies forward, pushing the boundaries of knowledge and understanding.

5. Resilience in the Face of Challenges:
Historical patterns of immigration reveal the resilience of societies in the face of challenges. Immigrant communities have often demonstrated adaptability and determination, contributing to the collective strength of their host nations during times of economic hardships, conflicts, or other crises.

6. Social and Cultural Integration Over Time:
Over generations, historical immigration patterns have showcased the capacity of societies to integrate and thrive

with diverse populations. While initial periods might witness challenges in assimilation, the long-term historical view reveals the establishment of harmonious coexistence, where different cultural, religious, and ethnic groups contribute to a shared national identity.

7. Enrichment of Culinary and Artistic Traditions:
The culinary and artistic landscapes of many societies bear the imprints of historical immigration. The fusion of diverse culinary traditions, for instance, has given rise to globally celebrated cuisines. Similarly, the

arts have been enriched by the contributions of immigrant artists, writers, musicians, and performers.

In conclusion, the historical contributions of immigration underscore a fundamental truth: societies thrive when they embrace diversity and recognize the positive impact of varied perspectives. The lessons of history demonstrate that immigration is not just a contemporary phenomenon but an enduring force that has shaped, strengthened, and enriched societies throughout the ages.

7

Humanitarian Considerations in Immigration: Upholding Basic Human Rights and Compassion

In the realm of immigration, a critical aspect that transcends political borders and policies is the humanitarian imperative. Providing refuge to individuals fleeing persecution or seeking a better life is not merely an act of benevolence; it is a commitment to upholding fundamental human rights and reflects the core values of compassion and solidarity.

1. Refuge from Persecution:

One of the primary tenets of humanitarian immigration is providing refuge to those facing persecution in their home countries. Individuals escaping war, violence, political oppression, or discrimination often seek asylum in countries that uphold human rights principles. Offering a safe haven is not only a moral obligation but also a demonstration of solidarity with those enduring hardship.

2. Protection of Vulnerable Populations:
Humanitarian immigration extends a protective umbrella to vulnerable populations, including

refugees, displaced persons, and those at risk due to their ethnicity, religion, or political beliefs. This commitment to safeguarding the most vulnerable aligns with the international community's shared responsibility to protect human dignity.

3. Pursuit of a Better Life: Beyond providing refuge, humanitarian immigration recognizes the inherent human desire for a better life. Individuals and families often embark on journeys to escape poverty, seeking opportunities for education, employment, and a chance to build a more secure future. Embracing immigrants with open arms acknowledges the shared aspiration for a dignified and improved quality of life.

4. Family Reunification: Humanitarian immigration includes policies that prioritize family reunification. Recognizing the importance of familial bonds, these policies aim to keep families together, acknowledging the emotional and psychological well-being derived from the support structures provided by close-knit family units.

5. Commitment to International Human Rights Standards:

Nations that embrace humanitarian immigration align themselves with international human rights standards and agreements. The Universal Declaration of Human Rights and other treaties emphasize the right to seek asylum, protection from persecution, and the principle of non-refoulement — not returning individuals to countries where they face serious threats to their lives or freedom.

6. Building Empathy and Global Solidarity:
Humanitarian immigration fosters empathy and global solidarity. By welcoming those in need,

societies contribute to a culture of compassion and understanding. This, in turn, promotes a shared commitment to addressing the root causes of displacement and working collaboratively to create a world where human rights are universally respected.

7. Diverse Contributions to Society:
Humanitarian immigrants often bring resilience, skills, and a strong work ethic to their new communities. Over time, their diverse contributions enrich the social, cultural, and economic fabric of the host nation, demonstrating that compassionate

immigration policies can yield positive outcomes for both the newcomers and the receiving society.

In conclusion, humanitarian considerations in immigration embody the principles of justice, compassion, and respect for human dignity. They reflect a commitment to a world where individuals are not defined by their nationality or circumstances but are valued as members of the broader human family, deserving of empathy, protection, and the opportunity to lead fulfilling lives.

Labor Market Dynamics and Immigration: Filling Gaps, Driving Economic Productivity

The intersection of immigration and labor market dynamics is a symbiotic relationship that has profound implications for economic growth. Immigrants frequently play a crucial role in filling gaps within the labor market, undertaking jobs that might be challenging to fill otherwise. Their contributions extend beyond mere employment; they become integral components of a dynamic workforce, enhancing overall economic productivity.

1. Addressing Labor Shortages:
One of the primary functions of immigrant labor is to address shortages in specific sectors. In industries such as agriculture, healthcare, hospitality, and construction, immigrants often take on roles that are physically demanding or require specific skill sets. This helps maintain a steady workforce, preventing disruptions in production and service provision due to a lack of available workers.

2. Flexibility and Adaptability:
Immigrants often demonstrate high levels of flexibility and adaptability in the labor market. Their willingness to take on a variety of roles, sometimes in response to shifting economic demands, contributes to the overall resilience of the workforce. This adaptability is particularly valuable in sectors that experience fluctuations in demand or seasonal variations.

3. Contribution to Economic Growth:
The presence of immigrants in the labor market contributes directly

to economic growth. By filling critical positions, they contribute to the production of goods and services, stimulating economic activity. This, in turn, has a multiplier effect, creating additional jobs and fostering a cycle of growth that benefits both the immigrant workforce and the broader economy.

4. Innovation and Entrepreneurship:
Immigrants often bring a spirit of innovation and entrepreneurship to the labor market. Many start their own businesses, contributing to the creation of jobs and economic development. The

entrepreneurial endeavors of immigrant communities can lead to the establishment of small and medium-sized enterprises, diversifying the economic landscape and fostering innovation.

5. Sustaining Vital Industries:
Certain industries heavily depend on immigrant labor to sustain their operations. For instance, in healthcare, immigrants often fill roles in nursing, caregiving, and other essential healthcare services. In the absence of immigrant workers, these critical industries might face challenges in meeting

the demands of a growing and aging population.

6. Supporting Skilled Labor Needs:
Immigrants also contribute significantly to skilled labor sectors, particularly in fields facing shortages of qualified professionals. From technology to engineering and healthcare, immigrants often bring specialized skills and expertise, addressing gaps in high-demand professions and contributing to advancements in these fields.

7. Social Security Contributions:

Immigrant workers contribute to social security systems through taxes and other payroll contributions. This financial input helps sustain social welfare programs, including retirement benefits and healthcare, benefiting both the immigrant workforce and the wider population.

In summary, the collaboration between immigrants and labor market dynamics is a powerful force driving economic productivity. Immigrants, by filling crucial roles, not only address immediate labor shortages but also contribute to the long-term economic health of the host nation. Recognizing and leveraging the skills and contributions of immigrant workers can lead to a more robust and resilient labor market, fostering sustainable economic growth.

9

Cultural Exchange through Immigration: Fostering Tolerance, Understanding, and Appreciation

Immigration serves as a dynamic force for cultural exchange, creating an environment where diverse perspectives, traditions, and ways of life converge. This intersection of cultures not only enriches the fabric of society but also plays a pivotal role in promoting tolerance, understanding, and a genuine appreciation for the diversity that defines our global community.

1. Mosaic of Traditions and Customs:
Immigration introduces a vibrant mosaic of traditions and customs. As individuals from different cultural backgrounds come together, they share their unique practices, rituals, and celebrations. This cultural tapestry transforms societies into living canvases,

where each thread contributes to a rich and diverse cultural landscape.

2. Breaking Down Stereotypes:
Interactions between people from various cultural backgrounds challenge and break down stereotypes. As individuals get to know one another on a personal level, preconceived notions give way to a deeper understanding of shared humanity. This process contributes to dispelling myths and fostering a more nuanced perspective on different cultures.

3. Language and Communication:
Language is a key element of cultural exchange. Immigrants bring with them a wealth of languages, each representing a unique way of expressing thoughts and emotions. The linguistic diversity that arises from immigration not only enhances communication but also fosters an appreciation for the beauty and intricacies of various languages.

4. Culinary Delights:
Food is a universal language, and immigration introduces a rich tapestry of culinary delights.

Immigrant communities often bring their traditional cuisines, offering a sensory journey that allows for a deeper understanding of cultural history, customs, and the significance of various ingredients.

5. Artistic Expressions: Immigrants contribute to the artistic landscape with a fusion of various artistic expressions. Whether in visual arts, literature, music, or dance, the amalgamation of diverse cultural influences leads to the creation of innovative and thought-provoking works. This artistic cross-pollination becomes a bridge for cultural understanding.

6. Celebration of Diversity:
Cultural exchange through immigration fosters a celebration of diversity. Instead of viewing differences as barriers, societies begin to appreciate the unique contributions each cultural group brings. This celebration becomes a source of strength, unity, and collective identity.

7. Fostering Tolerance and Empathy:
Interacting with people from different cultural backgrounds fosters tolerance and empathy.

Exposure to diverse perspectives encourages individuals to step outside their comfort zones, cultivating a broader worldview. This firsthand experience of diversity is a powerful antidote to prejudice and promotes a more inclusive and understanding society.

8. Bridging Generational Divides:
Cultural exchange through immigration also bridges generational divides. Older generations often retain cultural traditions from their countries of origin, and younger generations, born in or raised in the host

country, embody a fusion of cultures. This intergenerational exchange contributes to the evolution of cultural practices and creates a dynamic, ever-evolving cultural identity.

In conclusion, cultural exchange facilitated by immigration is a cornerstone of building harmonious and inclusive societies. It is a living testament to the idea that understanding and appreciating diverse ways of life can lead to stronger, more resilient communities that thrive on the richness of their collective cultural heritage.

10

Adaptability and Resilience: The Power of Immigration in Dynamic Societies

Societies that embrace immigration showcase a remarkable capacity for adaptability and resilience. By welcoming diverse populations, these societies not only adjust to changing demographics but also demonstrate a heightened ability to navigate the complexities of evolving global dynamics. The intersection of immigration, adaptability, and resilience becomes a driving force for societal growth and sustainability.

1. Demographic Flexibility: Immigration provides a dynamic response to shifting demographic patterns. Societies that actively embrace immigrants can more effectively manage demographic changes, such as aging populations or declining birth rates. The injection of new, often younger, individuals into the social fabric helps maintain a balanced age structure and supports the sustainability of social welfare systems.

2. Economic Adaptation:

Adaptability in the face of economic changes is a hallmark of societies that embrace immigration. Immigrant populations contribute to the labor force, adapting to the demands of various industries. Their diverse skills and willingness to fill gaps in the job market enhance a society's economic adaptability, fostering resilience in the face of economic fluctuations.

3. Global Connectivity: Societies that embrace immigration are inherently more globally connected. Immigrants often bring international perspectives, networks, and experiences. This interconnectedness positions the host society to adapt more readily to global changes, whether in trade, technology, or cultural shifts. The ability to navigate a globally connected world becomes a source of strength.

4. Cultural Dynamism: Immigrant communities infuse societies with cultural dynamism. The coexistence of diverse cultures creates an environment where different perspectives merge and evolve. This cultural fusion not only enhances the vibrancy of a society but also equips it with the cultural adaptability needed to engage with a rapidly changing world.

5. Social Innovation: Immigrants often bring innovative ideas and approaches, contributing to social innovation. Their unique experiences and perspectives encourage societies to explore new ways of problem-solving and community development. This social innovation becomes a crucial aspect of resilience, enabling societies to address emerging challenges effectively.

6. Integration Strategies:

Societies that successfully embrace immigration often develop effective integration strategies. These strategies go beyond mere coexistence and strive for the meaningful inclusion of immigrants in all aspects of society. Such inclusive practices contribute to social cohesion, creating a resilient framework that can withstand social tensions and promote unity.

7. Response to Global Challenges:
Immigrant-inclusive societies are better equipped to respond to global challenges. Whether facing environmental crises, public

health emergencies, or geopolitical shifts, these societies benefit from the diverse perspectives and skills brought by immigrants. This collective adaptability enhances the society's resilience in times of uncertainty.

8. Future-Ready Workforce: The adaptability of societies embracing immigration extends to the workforce. Immigrants often contribute to a more flexible and agile labor market, possessing skills that align with emerging industries and technologies. This future-ready workforce positions the society to thrive in an ever-evolving global economic landscape.

In conclusion, the adaptability and resilience demonstrated by societies that embrace immigration underscore the transformative power of diversity. These societies not only navigate the complexities of contemporary challenges more effectively but also position themselves as dynamic, inclusive, and resilient entities ready to embrace the opportunities of an ever-changing world.

Revitalizing Communities through Immigration: Infusing New Energy, Businesses, and Renewed Community Spirit

Immigration has the transformative power to breathe new life into declining or aging communities, offering a path to rejuvenation, economic vitality, and a renewed sense of community. As immigrants settle in these areas, they bring not only their diverse backgrounds but also a reservoir of energy, entrepreneurial spirit, and a commitment to community building.

1. Economic Stimulus:
One of the most tangible benefits immigrants bring to declining communities is economic revitalization. Immigrant entrepreneurs often establish businesses, create jobs, and stimulate local economies. Their contributions can lead to the development of new industries, diversification of economic activities, and increased local spending, creating a ripple effect that bolsters community prosperity.

2. Small Business Development:

Immigrants often engage in small business ventures, becoming catalysts for the creation of vibrant local markets. Establishing restaurants, shops, and service-oriented enterprises, they contribute to the development of a unique community identity while offering residents and visitors a diverse array of products and services.

3. Cultural Enrichment:
The infusion of diverse cultures by immigrant communities enriches the social fabric of declining areas. Cultural events, festivals, and celebrations become integral to community life,

fostering a sense of pride and identity. This cultural exchange not only revitalizes the community spirit but also attracts external interest and tourism.

4. Community Engagement and Social Cohesion:
Immigrants often actively engage in community life, participating in local activities, joining community organizations, and contributing to civic initiatives. This increased level of participation fosters social cohesion, breaking down barriers between new and existing residents. The sense of community renewal is amplified

as diverse voices come together to address common challenges and celebrate shared successes.

5. Rejuvenating Infrastructure:
The arrival of immigrant populations can be a catalyst for the rejuvenation of physical infrastructure. As communities grow, there is often a demand for new amenities, housing, and public spaces. This revitalization not only improves the quality of life for residents but also makes the community more attractive to potential newcomers and investors.

6. Workforce Development:
In communities facing demographic challenges, immigrants contribute to the workforce, helping address labor shortages. This is particularly crucial in sectors such as healthcare, education, and manufacturing, where skilled workers are in demand. The injection of new talent and skills contributes to the sustainability and growth of local industries.

7. Intergenerational Exchange:
Immigrant families often bring a multigenerational dynamic to communities. This

intergenerational exchange not only reinforces family values but also bridges the gap between older and younger residents. The transfer of knowledge, traditions, and skills becomes a cornerstone of community renewal, fostering a sense of continuity and shared history.

8. Entrepreneurial Energy: Immigrant communities are known for their entrepreneurial spirit. The establishment of businesses and startups by immigrants injects a fresh wave of entrepreneurial energy into declining areas. This not only creates economic opportunities but also cultivates an environment where innovation and risk-taking are embraced.

In conclusion, the revitalization of declining or aging communities through immigration is a dynamic process that goes beyond economic considerations. It involves the infusion of diverse cultures, the creation of new economic opportunities, and the establishment of a vibrant community spirit. When immigrants and existing residents collaborate, the result is a renewed sense of pride, identity, and shared prosperity that transforms the trajectory of the community for the better.

12

Social Services Impact: Immigrant Contributions through Taxes and Debunking Myths

Contrary to misconceptions, studies consistently reveal that immigrants often make substantial contributions to social services through taxes, challenging the unfounded notion that they are a burden on public resources. Understanding the intricate relationship between immigrants and social services provides a more accurate picture of their economic impact and underscores their positive role in supporting societal welfare.

1. Tax Contributions: Numerous studies indicate that immigrants contribute significantly to public finances through taxes. Whether through income taxes, property taxes, or consumption taxes, immigrants actively participate in funding government programs, including social services. Their financial contributions are integral to the functioning of social safety nets and public infrastructure.

2. Social Security and Other Contributions:
Immigrant workers, particularly those in their prime working years, contribute to social security and various programs. Through payroll taxes, they fund these essential programs that provide financial support and healthcare benefits to the elderly. This contribution becomes particularly valuable in addressing demographic challenges, such as an aging population.

3. Net Positive Fiscal Impact:
Research consistently shows that, on average, immigrants have a net positive fiscal impact. The taxes

they pay often exceed the public benefits they consume. This challenges the misconception that immigrants are a drain on public resources, highlighting their role as contributors to the fiscal health of the nation.

4. Economic Participation and Consumption:
Immigrants actively participate in the economy, contributing to its growth and generating economic activity. Through their labor, spending, and entrepreneurial activities, immigrants stimulate demand for goods and services. This, in turn, contributes to increased tax revenues that can be

allocated to fund social services and public infrastructure.

5. Education and Skill Levels:
The fiscal impact of immigrants is closely tied to their education and skill levels. Highly skilled immigrants, in particular, often contribute significantly to public coffers through higher income taxes. Additionally, their contributions extend to sectors that drive innovation, research, and economic growth, further supporting social services through indirect means.

6. Youthful Demographic Impact:
Many immigrants arrive in their working-age years, contributing to a more youthful demographic structure. This demographic advantage helps sustain social services by ensuring a steady influx of workers who contribute to the labor force and support social welfare systems. It counters demographic challenges associated with aging populations.

7. Entrepreneurial Contributions:
Immigrant entrepreneurs contribute to job creation, economic dynamism, and tax

revenues. By establishing businesses and driving innovation, they become key players in local and national economies. The economic ripple effect of entrepreneurial contributions extends to supporting social services and community development.

8. Debunking Myths and Fostering Inclusivity:
Understanding the positive fiscal impact of immigrants is crucial for debunking myths and fostering inclusivity. Dispelling misconceptions about immigrants being a burden on social services promotes a more informed and

constructive dialogue around immigration policies. It allows for the development of policies that embrace the economic and social contributions of immigrant communities.

In conclusion, the impact of immigrants on social services goes beyond mere consumption; it is a story of active participation, contribution, and net positive fiscal effects. Recognizing the valuable role immigrants play in supporting societal welfare challenges stereotypes and paves the way for policies that celebrate diversity and harness the economic vitality of immigrant communities.

13

Global Talent Pool Access through Immigration: Enriching Innovation and Expertise

Immigration serves as a gateway for countries to access a vast and diverse global talent pool. By attracting skilled individuals from around the world, nations can harness expertise that spans various sectors, including science, technology, academia, and beyond. This dynamic influx of talent not only enhances a country's capacity for innovation but also fosters a robust environment for intellectual exchange and economic growth.

1. Scientific Advancements: Immigration allows countries to attract top-notch scientists, researchers, and scholars. The exchange of knowledge and expertise leads to significant advancements in scientific fields. Many breakthroughs and discoveries are the result of collaborative efforts among scientists from different corners of the world, facilitated by inclusive immigration policies.

2. Technological Innovation:
Access to a global talent pool fosters technological innovation. Skilled immigrants often play pivotal roles in driving advancements in fields such as artificial intelligence, information technology, biotechnology, and engineering. Their diverse perspectives and expertise contribute to pushing the boundaries of what is possible, leading to the development of cutting-edge technologies.

3. Academic Excellence:
Universities and research institutions benefit immensely from immigration, as they attract

talented academics and students from diverse backgrounds. The cross-pollination of ideas and perspectives enriches the academic environment, leading to a higher level of excellence in research, teaching, and intellectual discourse.

4. Economic Competitiveness:
Countries that actively tap into the global talent pool enhance their economic competitiveness. Skilled immigrants contribute to the growth of key industries, driving economic expansion and ensuring that nations remain at the forefront of global markets. Their

expertise often leads to the establishment of successful businesses and startups, further contributing to economic vibrancy.

5. Diversity in Skill Sets: Immigration introduces a diverse array of skill sets to a country's workforce. This diversity is particularly valuable as it allows nations to address specific labor market needs, filling gaps with individuals possessing specialized knowledge and skills. The complementary nature of these skills enhances overall productivity and competitiveness.

6. Knowledge Exchange and Collaboration:
Skilled immigrants foster a culture of knowledge exchange and collaboration. By working alongside local talent, they contribute to a dynamic environment where ideas flow freely, leading to collaborative projects and initiatives. This collaborative spirit not only benefits specific industries but also contributes to the overall intellectual capital of a nation.

7. Addressing Skills Shortages:
In sectors facing skills shortages, immigration becomes a strategic

solution. Countries can attract skilled workers to fill critical roles in areas such as healthcare, engineering, and information technology. This proactive approach to addressing skills gaps ensures the continued growth and vitality of essential industries.

8. Cultural Diversity and Global Perspective:
Beyond their professional contributions, skilled immigrants bring cultural diversity and a global perspective to their host countries. This diversity enhances social and cultural experiences, fosters a climate of inclusivity,

and prepares societies to engage with an interconnected world.

In conclusion, the ability to access a global talent pool through immigration is a cornerstone of a nation's success in the modern era. By embracing skilled individuals from diverse backgrounds, countries position themselves as hubs of innovation, creativity, and economic competitiveness, ensuring they remain at the forefront of global progress.

14

Cultural Dynamism: Embracing Diversity for Creativity and Vibrancy

A diverse population is the heartbeat of cultural dynamism, injecting vitality and creativity into a country's social fabric. The rich tapestry of cultures, traditions, and identities that immigrants bring contributes to the evolution of a society, fostering hybrid identities, artistic expressions, and a vibrant cultural scene that reflects the kaleidoscope of human experiences.

1. Fusion of Traditions:

Immigration facilitates the fusion of diverse traditions, creating a melting pot of cultures within a nation. This fusion becomes a source of inspiration, where traditional practices from different parts of the world intersect, giving rise to new and innovative ways of celebrating festivals, rituals, and ceremonies.

2. Hybrid Identities:
The interaction of diverse cultural backgrounds results in the emergence of hybrid identities. Individuals navigate between the culture of their heritage and the culture of their adopted home, creating a unique blend that

reflects the complexities of identity in a multicultural society. These hybrid identities contribute to the richness and complexity of the cultural landscape.

3. Culinary Diversity:
One of the most tangible expressions of cultural dynamism is found in the culinary diversity brought by immigrants. Different cuisines and flavors converge, leading to a gastronomic explosion that not only tantalizes taste buds but also serves as a reflection of the cultural diversity within a nation.

4. Artistic Expressions and Creativity:
A diverse population serves as a wellspring of artistic expressions and creativity. Immigrant communities often bring unique art forms, music, dance, and literature that enrich the cultural scene. This infusion of creativity not only diversifies cultural offerings but also inspires local artists to explore new avenues of expression.

5. Language and Linguistic Diversity:
Immigrant populations contribute to linguistic diversity, with communities maintaining their

native languages. This linguistic richness becomes a bridge for cultural understanding and creates an environment where multilingualism is celebrated, fostering communication and appreciation across language boundaries.

6. Celebrating Differences: Cultural dynamism encourages the celebration of differences rather than their suppression. It promotes an inclusive society where various cultural expressions are acknowledged, respected, and embraced. This celebration of diversity becomes a powerful force for social cohesion and unity.

7. Global Perspectives:
A diverse population brings global perspectives to local communities. Immigrants often carry with them unique worldviews, experiences, and ways of thinking. This infusion of global perspectives challenges insular thinking, fostering a more open-minded and cosmopolitan society.

8. Vibrant Cultural Events:
The presence of diverse communities contributes to a calendar rich in cultural events.

Festivals, performances, and exhibitions showcasing the traditions and arts of various communities become integral parts of the cultural scene. These events not only entertain but also educate, fostering cross-cultural understanding.

9. Tolerance and Cultural Awareness:
Cultural dynamism encourages tolerance and cultural awareness. Exposure to different ways of life promotes understanding, dispels stereotypes, and challenges prejudices. This heightened cultural awareness creates a foundation for building

harmonious and inclusive societies.

In conclusion, cultural dynamism fueled by a diverse population is a driving force for creativity, innovation, and vibrancy within a nation. Embracing the richness of cultural diversity leads to a society that thrives on the interplay of different traditions, identities, and perspectives, creating a dynamic and evolving cultural landscape that reflects the beauty of human complexity.

15

Long-Term Economic Growth: The Integral Role of Immigrants in Productivity and Market Expansion

Immigrants, when effectively integrated into the workforce, play a pivotal role in fostering long-term economic growth. Their contributions extend beyond immediate benefits, influencing productivity, innovation, and the expansion of consumer markets. Embracing the economic potential of immigrants is not just a short-term advantage; it is a strategic investment in a nation's sustained prosperity.

1. Workforce Expansion and Productivity:
One of the primary drivers of long-term economic growth is the expansion of the workforce. Immigrants contribute to this expansion by bringing in additional labor, filling critical gaps in various sectors. Their participation in the labor market enhances overall productivity, contributing to increased output and economic efficiency.

2. Skills and Expertise:
Skilled immigrants often bring specialized skills and expertise that contribute to technological advancements and innovation.

This infusion of talent enhances a nation's competitiveness in the global economy. As immigrants integrate into industries requiring specific skills, they become catalysts for growth and development in key sectors.

3. Entrepreneurial Contributions:
Immigrant entrepreneurs are key players in driving long-term economic growth. Many immigrants establish businesses, creating jobs and stimulating economic activity. The entrepreneurial spirit they bring contributes to the dynamism of local economies, fostering

innovation and creating a conducive environment for the development of startups and small enterprises.

4. Consumption and Market Expansion:
Immigrants contribute to the expansion of consumer markets. As they become part of the workforce and society, their consumption patterns drive demand for goods and services. This increased demand not only sustains existing industries but also creates opportunities for the development of new markets and the diversification of economic activities.

5. Demographic Impact:
In nations facing demographic challenges, such as an aging population and declining birth rates, immigrants play a crucial role in maintaining a balanced age structure. Their presence ensures a steady stream of workers who can contribute to economic growth, support social welfare systems, and mitigate the economic implications of an aging workforce.

6. Innovation and Adaptability:
Immigrants, often exposed to diverse experiences and

perspectives, contribute to innovation and adaptability. Their ability to navigate different cultural and economic contexts fosters a culture of creativity within workplaces. This innovation is a driving force behind the development of new technologies, processes, and business models.

7. Regional Development and Revitalization:
Immigrants can contribute to the long-term economic growth of specific regions by settling in and revitalizing declining areas. Their entrepreneurial initiatives, skills, and labor force participation can

lead to the development of new industries, the rejuvenation of local economies, and the creation of sustainable communities.

8. Knowledge Transfer and Skills Development: Immigrants often bring a wealth of knowledge and skills from their home countries. This knowledge transfer not only benefits the receiving nation but also contributes to the development of a highly skilled and adaptable workforce. This, in turn, enhances the nation's capacity for innovation and long-term economic resilience.

In conclusion, recognizing and leveraging the economic contributions of immigrants is essential for sustained long-term growth. Embracing their role in expanding the workforce, driving innovation, and contributing to market expansion positions nations to thrive in an ever-evolving global economic landscape, ensuring prosperity for current and future generations.

16

Fulfilling Labor Market Gaps: Immigration as a Strategic Solution for Key Industries

Immigration serves as a strategic solution for addressing specific labor shortages in critical sectors, ensuring the sustained strength and resilience of industries such as healthcare, agriculture, and technology. By filling gaps in the labor market, immigrants contribute not only to the immediate needs of these industries but also to their long-term viability and growth.

1. Healthcare Sector Support: The healthcare industry often faces shortages of skilled professionals, including doctors, nurses, and other healthcare workers. Immigrants, especially those with medical training and expertise, play a crucial role in addressing these shortages. Their contributions bolster healthcare systems, improve patient care, and contribute to the overall well-being of communities.

2. Agricultural Labor:
In agriculture, seasonal labor demands can be challenging to meet with domestic workers alone. Immigrant labor, often willing to engage in physically demanding and seasonal work, fills these gaps, ensuring timely planting, harvesting, and maintenance of crops. This support is instrumental in

maintaining the productivity and competitiveness of the agricultural sector.

3. Technology and Innovation:
The technology sector frequently experiences shortages of skilled professionals with expertise in areas such as software development, data science, and engineering. Immigrant workers, often possessing advanced skills and qualifications, contribute to technological innovation. Their presence is vital for sustaining growth in a sector that plays a pivotal role in the modern economy.

4. Addressing STEM (Science, Technology, Engineering, and Mathematics) Gaps:
Many countries face shortages of professionals in STEM fields, which are critical for advancements in science and technology. Immigrant workers, particularly those with advanced degrees in STEM disciplines, contribute to research, development, and innovation, ensuring that nations remain at the forefront of scientific progress.

5. Construction and Skilled Trades:

The construction industry and skilled trades often experience fluctuations in demand for labor. Immigrant workers, including those with skills in carpentry, plumbing, and electrical work, fill these gaps, contributing to the development of infrastructure and the growth of the construction sector.

6. Service Industries:
In service industries, such as hospitality and caregiving, immigrant workers play a significant role. Their contributions in roles like housekeeping, food service, and caregiving address the labor needs

of these sectors. Immigrant workers often bring a strong work ethic and adaptability, contributing to the overall success of service industries.

7. Economic Impact on Local Communities:
Fulfilling labor market gaps through immigration has a positive economic impact on local communities. The presence of immigrant workers stimulates economic activity, contributing to local businesses and services. This economic ripple effect strengthens community resilience and fosters a dynamic and diverse local economy.

8. Long-Term Workforce Sustainability:
Immigration addresses immediate labor shortages while contributing to the long-term sustainability of the workforce. By filling critical roles, immigrants support the continuity of industries, preventing disruptions that could occur if labor gaps persist. This long-term stability is essential for the overall health and growth of key sectors.

In conclusion, immigration emerges as a strategic and indispensable solution for fulfilling labor market gaps in key industries. By strategically integrating immigrants into sectors facing shortages, nations can ensure the vitality, growth, and sustainability of industries that form the backbone of their economies.

17

Entrepreneurship and Small Business Growth: Immigrant Contributions to Economic Development and Job Creation

The entrepreneurial spirit of immigrants has been a driving force behind the success of many businesses, contributing significantly to overall economic development and job creation. Across various industries, immigrants bring innovation, determination, and a unique perspective that not only fosters the growth of their own enterprises but also enriches the economic landscape of their host countries.

1. Startup Prowess:
Immigrants have a notable track record of founding successful startups. Their entrepreneurial ventures span a wide range of sectors, including technology, healthcare, retail, and service industries. Many renowned

companies, both large and small, owe their inception to the vision and initiative of immigrant entrepreneurs.

2. Job Creation: Entrepreneurial endeavors initiated by immigrants result in substantial job creation. As immigrant-owned businesses expand, they hire local employees, contributing to lower unemployment rates and supporting the economic well-being of the community. The collective impact of immigrant entrepreneurs on job markets is a testament to their role as engines of employment growth.

3. Economic Stimulus:
Immigrant entrepreneurs stimulate economic activity by establishing and growing businesses. These businesses generate revenue, contribute to local and national tax bases, and create a multiplier effect by fostering additional economic transactions. The economic stimulus generated by immigrant-led enterprises benefits not only the entrepreneurs themselves but also the broader community.

4. Industry Diversity:
The diversity of immigrant backgrounds often translates into

a diverse array of business ideas and ventures. Immigrant entrepreneurs bring unique perspectives and insights, leading to the creation of businesses that cater to a wide range of consumer needs. This diversity contributes to a more resilient and adaptable economy.

5. Niche Markets and Innovation:
Many immigrant entrepreneurs identify and address niche markets that might have been overlooked, leading to innovation and the development of specialized products and services. This entrepreneurial innovation

not only meets specific consumer demands but also enhances the competitiveness of the business landscape.

6. Cultural Contributions to Business:
The fusion of cultural influences often characterizes immigrant-led businesses. From culinary enterprises to fashion and entertainment, immigrant entrepreneurs infuse their businesses with cultural richness. This not only adds uniqueness to the business landscape but also attracts diverse customer bases, contributing to the economic vibrancy of communities.

7. Community Engagement:
Immigrant entrepreneurs frequently engage with their local communities, creating a sense of connection and shared prosperity. These entrepreneurs often sponsor community events, support local initiatives, and actively participate in the civic life of their adopted home. This community engagement reinforces the positive impact of immigrant businesses beyond the economic realm.

8. Global Business Networks:

Immigrant entrepreneurs often leverage global business networks. Their connections to international markets and suppliers can facilitate trade and collaboration, contributing to the globalization of local economies. This interconnectedness positions communities with immigrant-led businesses as players in the broader global marketplace.

9. Overcoming Challenges: Many immigrant entrepreneurs face and overcome unique challenges in the business landscape, showcasing resilience and determination. These success stories inspire others and contribute to the narrative of immigrants as valuable contributors to the entrepreneurial spirit of their host nations.

In conclusion, immigrant entrepreneurship is a dynamic force that not only shapes the economic landscape of a country but also plays a crucial role in job creation, community development, and overall economic prosperity. Recognizing and supporting the entrepreneurial endeavors of immigrants is a strategic investment in the growth and vibrancy of local and national economies.

18

Language Skills: Multilingual Populations and the Global Advantage of Immigration

Immigration contributes significantly to the development of multilingual populations within a country, offering a valuable resource that enhances its ability to engage in global business, diplomacy, and cultural exchange. The linguistic diversity brought by immigrants becomes a strategic asset, fostering effective communication and collaboration in an interconnected world.

1. Global Business Communication:
In the realm of global business, language skills are a valuable asset. Immigrants often bring proficiency in multiple languages, facilitating communication with international clients, partners, and customers. This linguistic versatility not only opens up new markets but also fosters stronger business relationships by bridging linguistic and cultural gaps.

2. Diplomatic Relations and International Collaboration:
Effective diplomacy relies on clear and nuanced communication. Multilingual

populations resulting from immigration contribute to a country's diplomatic prowess by providing individuals with the language skills necessary to navigate international negotiations, treaties, and collaborations. This linguistic diversity strengthens a nation's position on the global stage.

3. Cultural Exchange and Soft Power:
Language is a key component of cultural exchange, and immigrant communities contribute to a country's soft power by fostering linguistic diversity. The ability to communicate in multiple

languages enables a nation to share its cultural richness with the world and engage in meaningful dialogue with diverse global audiences. This exchange builds bridges of understanding and appreciation between nations.

4. Improved Intercultural Understanding:
Multilingual populations promote improved intercultural understanding. Immigrants, often fluent in their native languages, facilitate a deeper appreciation of their cultures and perspectives. This understanding is crucial for building trust, resolving conflicts, and promoting peaceful

coexistence in a world characterized by diverse cultures and backgrounds.

5. Educational Advantages: Children growing up in multilingual communities often have the advantage of being exposed to different languages from an early age. This exposure enhances their cognitive abilities, including problem-solving and creativity. Moreover, it equips them with the skills needed to navigate an increasingly interconnected global job market.

6. Global Talent Attraction:

Countries that embrace linguistic diversity become more attractive to global talent. Immigrants, knowing they can maintain their language and cultural ties, are more likely to choose destinations that value and support linguistic diversity. This attraction of global talent contributes to the economic and cultural vibrancy of the host nation.

7. Linguistic Adaptability in a Changing World:
A multilingual population demonstrates adaptability in a rapidly changing world. As global dynamics shift, countries with diverse language skills are better

equipped to navigate emerging challenges, participate in evolving economic landscapes, and seize opportunities in different regions of the world.

8. Innovation and Cross-Cultural Collaboration: Language skills are essential for fostering innovation through cross-cultural collaboration. Immigrant communities, with their diverse linguistic backgrounds, provide a fertile ground for the exchange of ideas and the development of innovative solutions that draw on a range of cultural perspectives.

In conclusion, the linguistic diversity resulting from immigration is a strategic asset that positions a country for success in the global arena. It not only facilitates international business and diplomacy but also enriches cultural exchange, fostering a more interconnected and harmonious world where diverse linguistic talents contribute to the collective progress of humanity.

19

International Relations: Embracing Immigrants as a Catalyst for Global Cooperation

The way a nation welcomes and integrates immigrants has far-reaching implications for its international relations. Embracing immigrants fosters positive diplomatic ties and showcases a commitment to shared humanity, contributing to a global environment characterized by cooperation, understanding, and solidarity.

1. Diplomatic Goodwill:
A nation's approach to immigration serves as a reflection of its values and principles. By welcoming immigrants, a country signals its commitment to

inclusivity, diversity, and humanitarian values. This stance generates diplomatic goodwill, enhancing its reputation on the global stage and promoting positive relationships with other nations.

2. Soft Power and Global Influence:
Soft power, the ability to influence others through attraction and persuasion, is a crucial aspect of international relations. A country that embraces immigrants and values diversity enhances its soft power. This, in turn, amplifies its global influence, as nations with inclusive policies are

often viewed as more
approachable, cooperative, and
forward-thinking.

3. Cultural Diplomacy:
Immigrants bring with them a
wealth of cultural diversity. By
embracing this diversity, a nation
engages in cultural diplomacy on
an unprecedented scale. This
cultural exchange fosters
understanding and appreciation
between nations, transcending
political differences and
contributing to the creation of a
more interconnected and
harmonious world.

4. Shared Humanity and Global Cooperation:
Welcoming immigrants reinforces the idea of shared humanity, transcending borders and emphasizing the interconnectedness of the global community. This commitment to our common humanity lays the foundation for enhanced international cooperation on issues ranging from human rights and environmental challenges to global health crises.

5. Diplomatic Leverage:
A nation that values immigration and diversity gains diplomatic leverage. By championing

inclusivity, it positions itself as a leader in the global effort to address shared challenges. This diplomatic standing can be leveraged to foster collaborative initiatives, negotiate partnerships, and contribute to the resolution of complex international issues.

6. Addressing Global Disparities:
The willingness to welcome immigrants often aligns with a broader commitment to addressing global disparities. Nations that recognize the socio-economic challenges faced by many immigrants demonstrate empathy and a sense of

responsibility. This shared commitment to reducing global inequalities becomes a basis for cooperative initiatives and partnerships.

7. Human Rights Advocacy: Immigration policies that prioritize the well-being and rights of immigrants signal a commitment to human rights. This advocacy for human rights resonates globally, earning the respect and cooperation of nations that share similar values. It positions the nation as a champion for justice and equality on the international stage.

8. Multilateral Collaboration:
Countries that embrace immigrants are more likely to engage in multilateral collaborations. These collaborations, whether in the form of international treaties, agreements, or joint initiatives, contribute to a more interconnected and cooperative world. Shared experiences and diverse perspectives brought by immigrants enrich the collaborative efforts of nations.

9. Resilience in the Face of Global Challenges:
A nation with a diverse and inclusive population is better

equipped to face global challenges. Whether addressing climate change, public health crises, or economic uncertainties, the resilience demonstrated through inclusive immigration policies strengthens a country's ability to navigate the complexities of an interconnected world.

In conclusion, embracing immigrants is not merely a domestic policy but a powerful tool for shaping positive international relations. By fostering a commitment to shared humanity and global cooperation, nations can build bridges, enhance diplomatic ties, and contribute to the creation of a more harmonious and interconnected world.

20

Civic Engagement: Immigrant Contributions to Democracy and Community Development

The integration of immigrants into the fabric of society often leads to robust civic engagement, where individuals actively participate in democratic processes and contribute to the development of their communities. Immigrants, once integrated, become valuable contributors to the democratic discourse, community building, and the overall vibrancy of civic life.

1. Voting and Political Participation:
Once granted the opportunity to participate in the democratic process, immigrants often become enthusiastic voters and active participants in political activities. Their diverse perspectives and experiences enrich political discussions, contributing to a more comprehensive representation of community interests.

2. Community Advocacy and Activism:
Immigrants frequently engage in community advocacy and activism, addressing issues that impact not only their own communities but the broader society. Whether advocating for social justice, education, or healthcare reform, their involvement amplifies diverse voices within the civic sphere.

3. Leadership and Representation:
As immigrants become integrated into society, they often take on leadership roles within their communities. This includes

participation in local government, community organizations, and civic boards. Their representation contributes to a more inclusive decision-making process, ensuring a broader range of perspectives are considered.

4. Community Service and Volunteering:
A commitment to community development often drives immigrants to actively participate in community service and volunteering. They contribute their time, skills, and resources to various causes, fostering a sense of solidarity and mutual support within their neighborhoods.

5. Cultural Events and Celebrations:
Immigrants frequently organize and participate in cultural events and celebrations that contribute to the richness of civic life. These events not only preserve cultural heritage but also provide opportunities for cross-cultural exchange, fostering understanding and unity within diverse communities.

6. Educational Involvement:
Immigrant parents often play an active role in the educational experiences of their children. Their engagement with schools,

parent-teacher associations, and educational initiatives contributes to the overall improvement of educational systems and outcomes.

7. Economic Development Initiatives:
Immigrants, recognizing the interconnectedness of economic well-being and civic life, engage in economic development initiatives. This includes starting businesses, investing in local economies, and participating in initiatives that create job opportunities and promote financial stability within communities.

8. Bridging Social Gaps:
Immigrants, by actively participating in civic life, contribute to bridging social gaps within communities. Their involvement in various activities and organizations fosters social cohesion, breaks down cultural barriers, and creates a more integrated and harmonious society.

9. Participatory Democracy:
Civic engagement by immigrants is a manifestation of participatory democracy. As active contributors to public discussions, policy advocacy, and community

initiatives, immigrants enrich the democratic process by ensuring a diversity of voices is heard and considered in decision-making.

10. Civic Education and Integration Programs:
Efforts to integrate immigrants often include civic education programs, which equip individuals with the knowledge and skills necessary to engage in civic life. These programs empower immigrants to navigate the complexities of democratic processes, fostering informed and active citizenship.

In conclusion, the civic engagement of immigrants is a testament to their commitment to democratic values, community well-being, and the shared responsibilities of citizenship. As active participants in civic life, immigrants contribute to the vitality and resilience of societies, enriching the democratic experience for everyone.

www.ingramcontent.com/pod-product-compliance
Lightning Source LLC
Chambersburg PA
CBHW070945260726
48661CB00003B/1125